Audio Access Included - Recorded Accompaniments Online

THE DEVELOPING CLASSICAL SINGER - MEZZO-SOPRANO

Songs by British and American Composers

THE DEVELOPING
Classical Singer

MEZZO-SOPRANO

ISBN 978-1-4950-9415-6

To access companion recorded piano accompaniments online, visit:
www.halleonard.com/mylibrary

Enter Code
4715-1992-0469-2053

BOOSEY & HAWKES

AN IMAGEM COMPANY

DISTRIBUTED BY
HAL•LEONARD®
7777 W. BLUEMOUND RD. P.O. BOX 13819 MILWAUKEE, WI 53213

www.boosey.com
www.halleonard.com

PREFACE

The Developing Classical Singer was compiled from the rich choices in the Boosey & Hawkes catalogue, with songs in English by British and American composers. The selection of songs is for the teenage voice, or an early level collegiate singer, or an adult amateur taking voice lessons.

The songs were chosen with some specific issues in mind: vocal ranges that are not extreme, and musical challenges that are manageable for a singer at this level. Beyond art song, we have included folksong arrangements, such as those by Aaron Copland and Benjamin Britten, which are fully composed in the spirit of an art song, designed for a classical voice.

There are different compilations for each voice type: soprano, mezzo-soprano, tenor and baritone. Some cornerstone songs are in all volumes, because of their beauty and appropriateness for any voice. These include Britten's "O Waly, Waly"; Ireland's "Spring Sorrow"; Britten's realization of Purcell's "I attempt from love's sickness to fly"; Quilter's "Weep you no more"; and Vaughan Williams' "Bright is the ring of words." Beyond that, it is the editor's subjective choice about which songs work best for each voice type. Gender is certainly a factor in this, but also just the vocal sound and color of a song. Original keys of the songs were considered, but since nearly every composer of art song is not opposed to transposition, original keys were not a confining factor in which volume a song lands.

A few pedagogical reasons for assigning songs to students, though many other topics could be addressed:

Agility
I attempt from love's sickness to fly
Sephestia's Lullaby
A Spring Song

Breath Support for a Long Phrase
Dirge
A Lullaby
The Nurse's Song
O Waly, Waly
Sail on, sail on
The sky above the roof

Building an Expressive Legato Phrase
At the River
Dream Valley
If music be the food of love
Love
Love went a-riding
O Waly, Waly
Simple Gifts
Spring Sorrow
Weep you no more

Expanding Vocal Range
Love's Philosophy
The Nurse's Song
The world feels dusty

Dynamic Contrasts
The Little Horses
The sky above the roof

Sensitively Expressing Poetry
Bright is the ring of words
Dream Valley
Heart, we will forget him
Little Elegy
The world feels dusty

Building Musicianship
Dirge
I hate music!
It was a lover and his lass
Love
Sephestia's Lullaby

Personality and Storytelling
I hate music!
Linden Lea
Love's Philosophy

There are some songs for those voices that naturally and easily sing higher in the range, though all the songs were chosen with student voices in mind. The highest vocal note in this entire book is the high F-sharp in "The world feels dusty" and "Love's Philosophy." Beyond the music, singers should learn to consider the words carefully, understanding them apart from the music, and pondering what the composer intended with the setting of the words to notes. This is the way into true personal expression, and is the real secret to becoming an artist as a performer of art song.

Richard Walters
Editor

CONTENTS

Pianists on the recordings: [1] Laura Ward, [2] Brendan Fox, [3] Richard Walters

for Nicholas Di Virgilio

Dirge

from *Six Elizabethan Songs*

original key: a minor 3rd higher

WILLIAM SHAKESPEARE

DOMINICK ARGENTO

I hate music!

from *I Hate Music!*

original key: a major third higher

Words and Music by
LEONARD BERNSTEIN

Love went a-riding

original key: a minor 3rd higher

MARY E. COLERIDGE

FRANK BRIDGE

Allegro energico

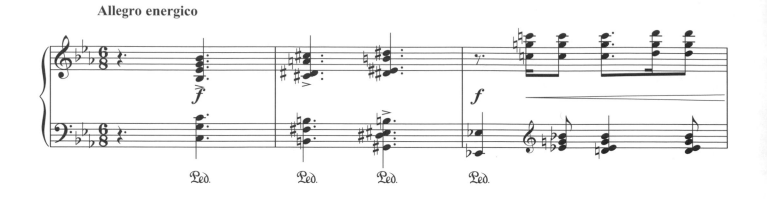

Love _____ went a-

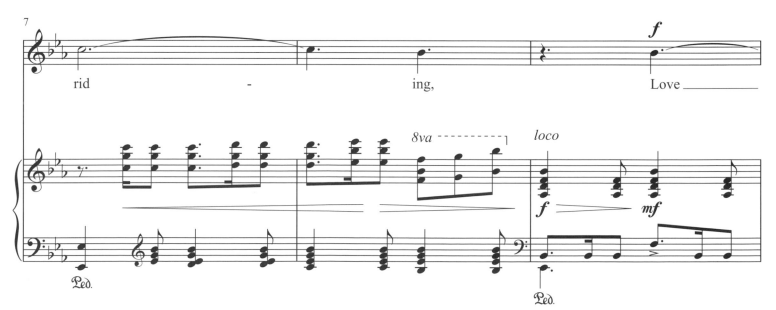

rid - ing, Love _____

went a - rid - ing o - ver the

earth, _____ On Peg - a-sus he

rode. _____ The

flowers _____ be - fore him sprang _____ to

birth, _____ And the fro - zen riv - ers

flowed. _____

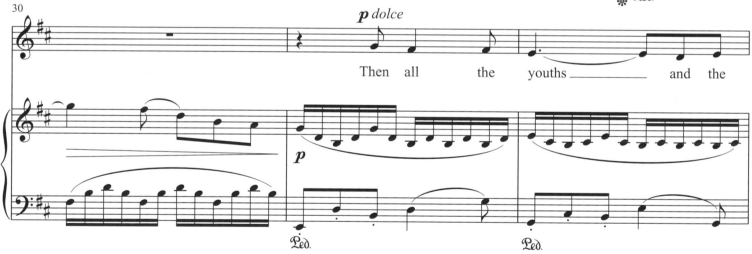

Then all the youths _____ and the

maid - ens cried, _____ "Stay here _____ with

ride   has   wings."

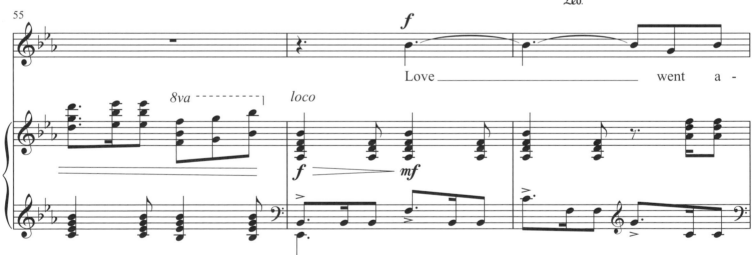

Love _____ went a -

rid - ing,   Love _____ went a -

rid - ing o - ver the earth, _____

On Peg - a - sus

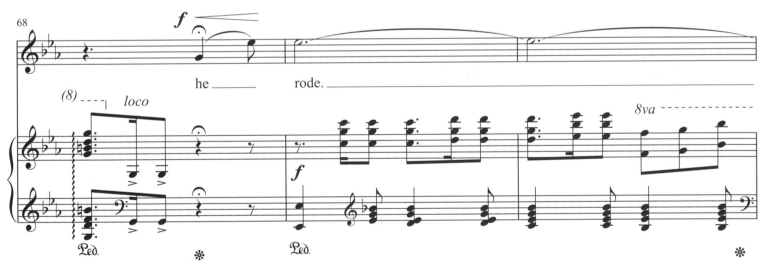

he _____ rode. _____

The Nurse's Song

from *A Charm of Lullabies*

original key

JOHN PHILIP

BENJAMIN BRITTEN
Op. 41, No. 5

Andante piacevole

Lull - a - by ba - by, Lull - a - by - la - by ba - by,

Thy nurse will tend thee as du - ly as may be. Lull - a - by

a tempo ... *molto espr.*

ba - by! ___ Be still, my sweet sweet-ing, no long - er do

p espress.

con Ped.

cry; Sing lull - a - by ba - by, lull - a - by ba - by. ___

pp dolce

Let dol - ours be fleet - ing, I fan - cy thee, I, _____ To

rock and to lull thee I will not de - lay me. Lull - a - by

ba - by _____ Lull - a - by - la - by - la - by ba - by, _____

Thy nurse will tend thee as du - ly as may be _____ lull - a - by - la -

by - la - by ba - by   The gods be thy shield and com - fort in

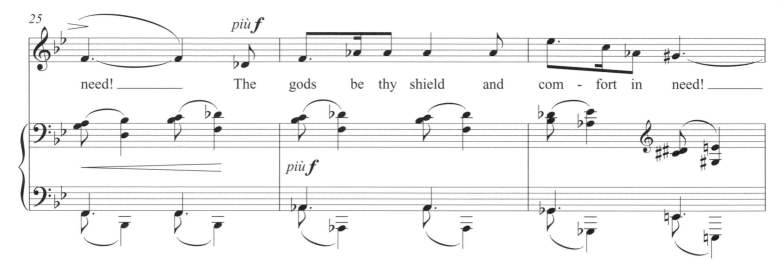

need! _____ The gods be thy shield and com - fort in need! _____

Sing lull - a - by ba - by _____   Lull - a - by - la - by

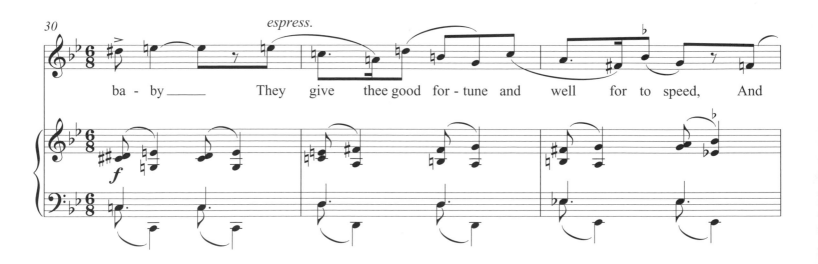

ba - by _____ They give thee good for - tune and well for to speed,   And

this to de - sire ___ I will not de - lay me. This to de - sire ___ I

will not de - lay me.

più dim.

Lull - a - by - ba - by lull - a - by - la - by ba - by, Thy nurse will tend thee as

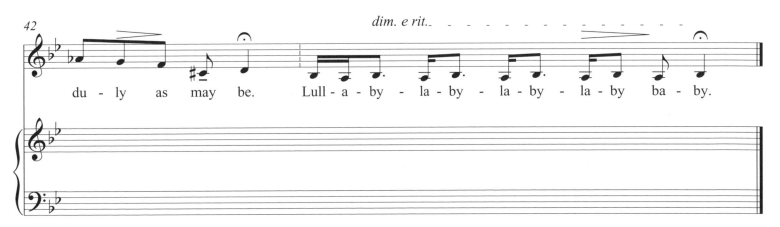

du - ly as may be. Lull - a - by - la - by - la - by - la - by ba - by.

[Dec. 1947-Aldeburgh]

O Waly, Waly

from Somerset (Cecil Sharp)*
from *Folksong Arrangements Volume 3: British Isles*
original key: a major 2nd higher

Arranged by
BENJAMIN BRITTEN

O, love is hand - some and love is fine, and love's a

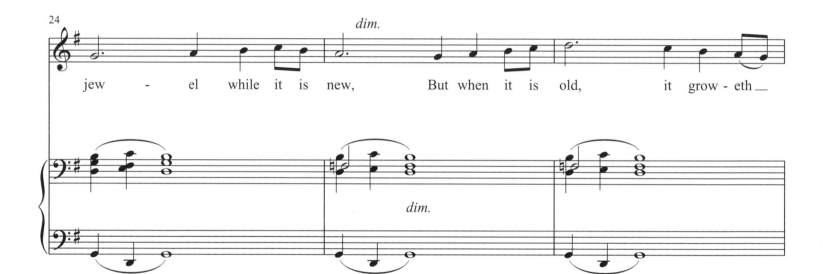

jew - el while it is new, But when it is old, it grow - eth

cold, and fades a - way like morn - ing dew.

This page intentionally left blank to facilitate page turns.

Sail on, sail on
(The Humming of the Ban)

from *Folksong Arrangements Volume 4: Moore's Irish Melodies*

original key: a major 3rd higher

from Thomas Moore's *Irish Melodies*

Arranged by
BENJAMIN BRITTEN

12

smil - ing bil - low seems to say "Tho' death be - neath our sur - face be, Less
if some des - ert land we meet, Where nev - er yet false - heart - ed men Pro -

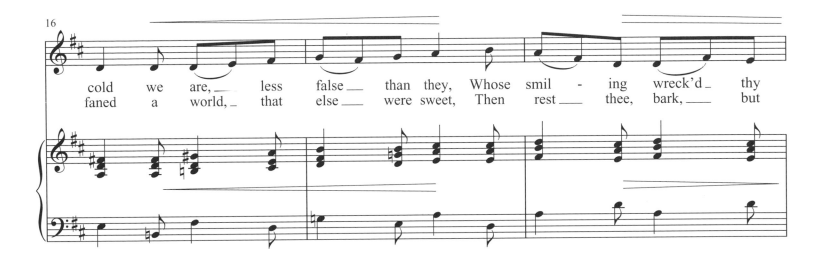

16

cold we are, ___ less false ___ than they, Whose smil - ing wreck'd ___ thy
faned a world, ___ less that else ___ were sweet, Then rest ___ thee, bark, ___ but

19

1.
hopes and thee."

2.
not till

p

p *dim.*

23

then.

dying away - - - - - - - - - - - - - - - - - - -

Sephestia's Lullaby

from *A Charm of Lullabies*

original key

ROBERT GREENE

BENJAMIN BRITTEN
Op. 41, No. 3

Such a boy by him and me, _____ He was glad,

I was woe; For - tune chang - ed made him so, When he left his

pret - ty boy, Last his sor - row, first his joy. _____

Weep not, my wan - ton, smile ___ up - on my knee;

When thou art old there's grief e-nough for thee.

Doppio movimento (allegretto)

leggiero

The wan - ton smiled, fa - ther wept,

Moth - er cried, ba - by leapt; More he crow - èd, more we cried,

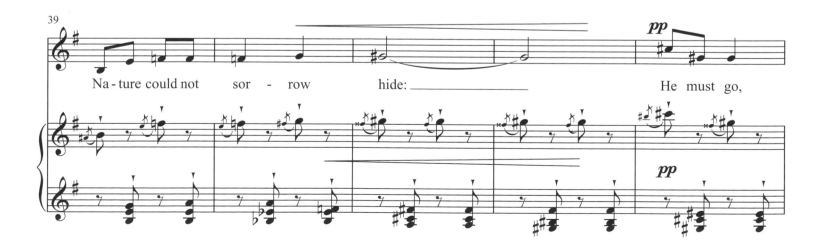

Na - ture could not sor - row hide: He must go,

he must kiss Child and moth-er, ba-by bliss, For he left his pret-ty boy,

Fa-ther's sor-row, fa-ther's joy. _____ Weep not, my

wan-ton, Smile up-on my knee, When thou art old _____ There's grief e-nough for

Doppio movimento (allegretto)

thee.

At the River

(Hymn Tune)

from *Old American Songs, Second Set*

original key

Arranged by
AARON COPLAND

riv - er, Ga - ther with the saints __ by the riv - er That

flows by the throne of __ God. _____ *cresc.*

ff

Soon we'll reach the shin - ing

(cresc.) **ff**

meno f

riv - er, Soon our pil - grim-age will cease, _____

meno f

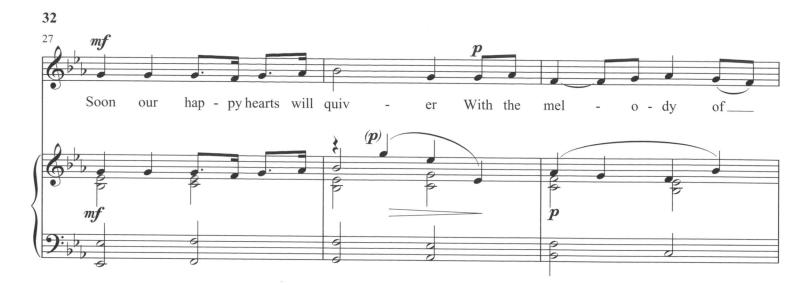

The Little Horses
(Lullaby)
from *Old American Songs, Second Set*
original key

Arranged by
AARON COPLAND

To Marcelle de Manziarly

Heart, we will forget him
from *Twelve Poems of Emily Dickinson*
original key: a major 2nd higher

EMILY DICKINSON

AARON COPLAND

* Grace note on the beat

Simple Gifts

(Shaker Song)

from *Old American Songs, First Set*

original key: a minor 2nd higher

Arranged by
AARON COPLAND

To Alexei Haieff

The world feels dusty

from *Twelve Poems of Emily Dickinson*
original key

EMILY DICKINSON

AARON COPLAND

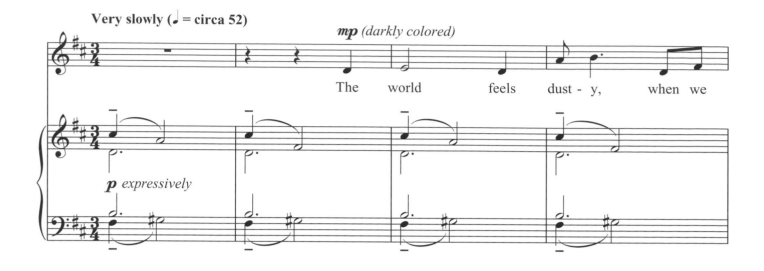

It was a lover and his lass

from *Let Us Garlands Bring*

original key

WILLIAM SHAKESPEARE*

GERALD FINZI
Op. 18, No. 5

*The 1623 Folio text is here collated with the version in Thomas Morley's "The First book of Ayres" 1600.

o'er the green corn - field did pass In
spring time, _____ the on - ly pret - ty
ring time, _____ When birds do
sing, _____ hey ding a ding a ding; Sweet lov - ers

col Ped.

love _____ the spring. _____

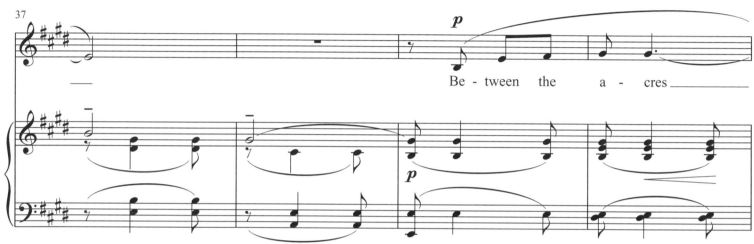

Be - tween the a - cres _____

___ of the rye, _____ With a

hey, and a ho, and a hey ___ non - i - no, _____

These pret-ty coun-try folks would lie, In spring time,_____ the on-ly pret-ty ring time,_____ When birds do sing,_____ hey ding a ding a ding; Sweet

lov - ers   love _____   the   spring. _____

poco ritard.

dim.

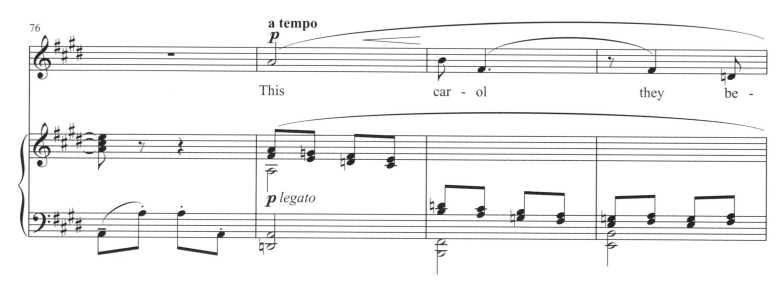

a tempo

This   car - ol   they   be -

p legato

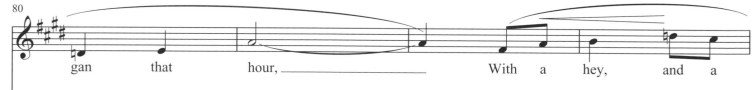

gan   that   hour, _____   With   a   hey,   and   a

When birds do sing, _____ hey ding a ding a ding; Sweet

lov - ers love _____ the spring. _____

And there - fore take the pres - ent

time, _____ With a hey, and a ho, and a

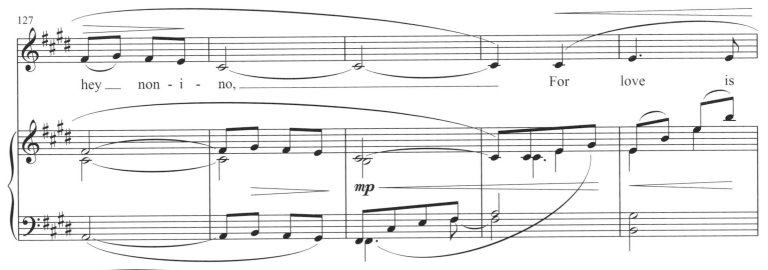

hey __ non - i - no, _____ For love is

crown - ed with the prime In spring time, _____

the on - ly pret - ty ring time, _____

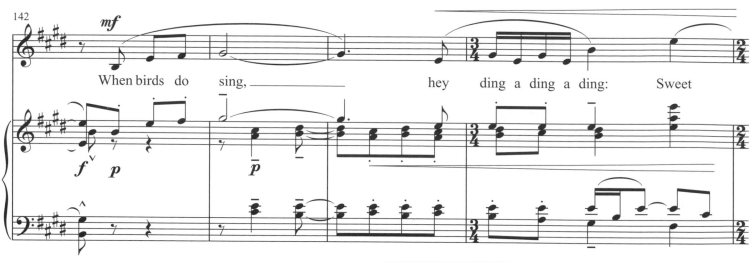

When birds do sing, _____ hey ding a ding a ding: Sweet

lov - ers love _____

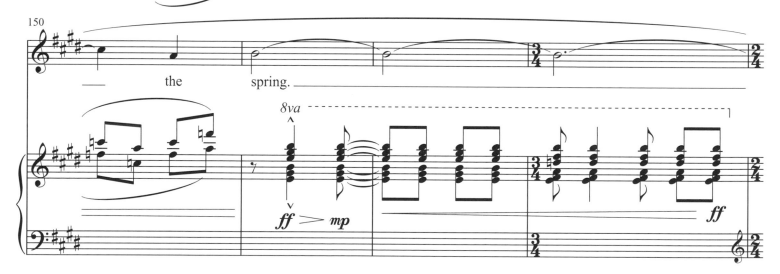

the spring. _____

Spring Sorrow

original key

RUPERT BROOKE

JOHN IRELAND

This Poem is reprinted from "1914 and other Poems" by Rupert Brooke,
by permission of the Literary Executor and Messrs Sidgwick and Jackson Ltd.

pain. My __ heart all Win - ter lay so numb, The

poco cresc.

earth so dead and frore, That I nev - er thought __ the

Spring would come, Or my heart wake an - y more. But

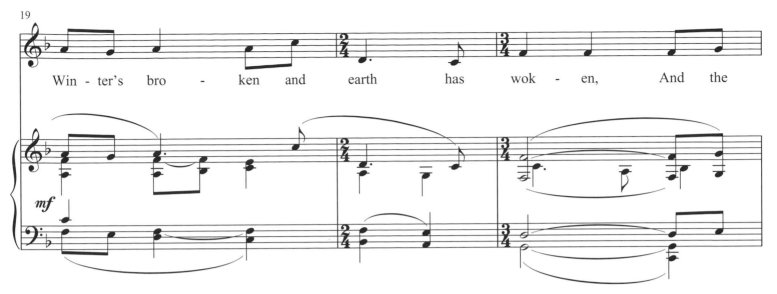

Winter's bro - ken and earth has wok - en, And the

small birds cry a - gain; And the haw - thorn hedge __ puts forth its buds And my

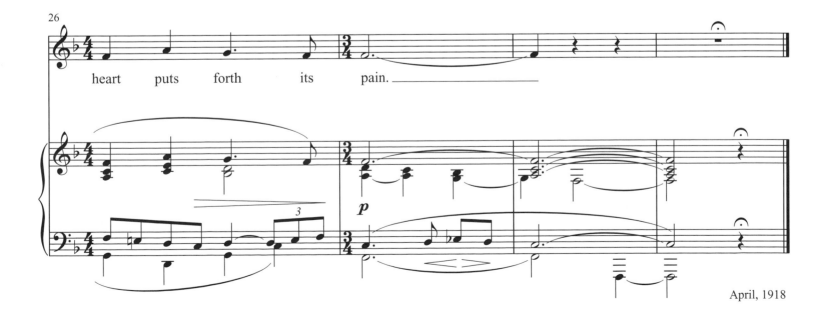

heart puts forth its pain. _____

April, 1918

A Spring Song

original key: a major 2nd higher

WILLIAM SHAKESPEARE
from *As You Like It*

C. HUBERT H. PARRY

It was a lov - er ___ and his lass, With a

hey and a ho, and a hey ___ no - ni - no! That o'er the green ___ corn -

field did pass In the spring - time, the on - ly pret - ty

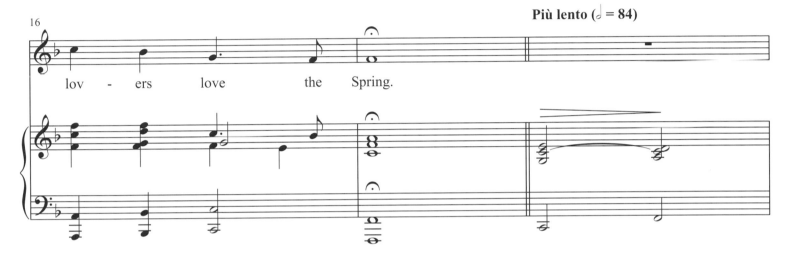

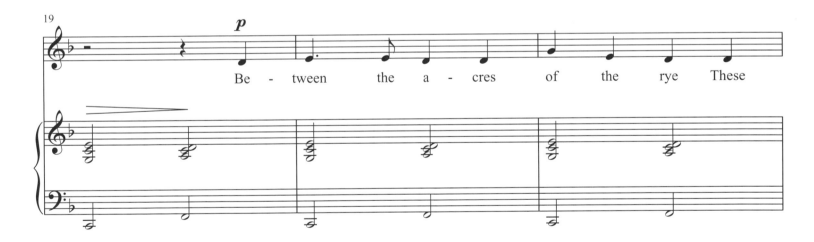

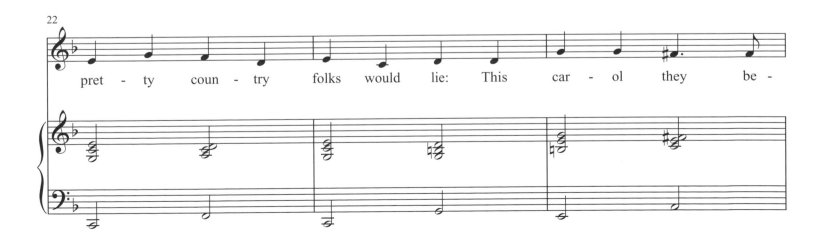

gan that hour, How that life was but a flow'r,

How that life was but a flow'r.

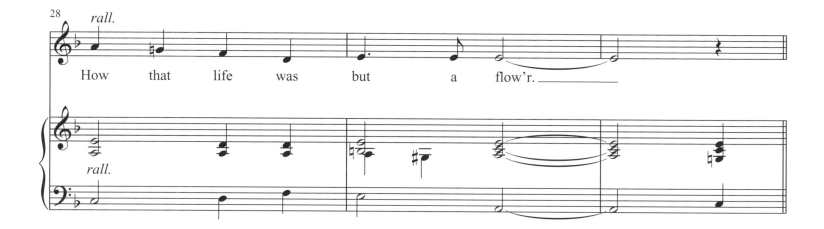

And there - fore take the pre - sent time With a

hey and a ho, and a hey no - ni - no! For love is crown - ed

with the prime, In spring - time, the on - ly pret - ty

ring - time, When birds do sing Hey ding a ding, Sweet

lov - ers love the Spring.

I attempt from love's sickness to fly

from *Five Songs* (Orpheus Britannicus)

original key: a major 3rd higher

JOHN DRYDEN
and ROBERT HOWARD

HENRY PURCELL
realized by
BENJAMIN BRITTEN

For love has more pow'r and less mer - cy than fate, To make us seek

ru - in, to make us seek ru - in and love those that hate. I at-

tempt from love's sick - ness to fly in vain, Since

I am my - self my own fe - ver, since I am my - self my own fe - ver and pain.

If music be the food of love

(1st Version)

from *Six Songs* (Orpheus Britannicus)
original key: a perfect 4th higher

HENRY HEVENINGHAM

HENRY PURCELL
realized by
BENJAMIN BRITTEN

feast - ed ___ are and all my sens - es ___ feast - ed ___ are, Tho' yet _ the treat _ is

on - ly ___ sound, Sure I must per - ish by your charms un -

less you save _____ me _ in your _ arms Sure I must per - ish

by your charms un - less you save _____ me _ in your _ arms.

To my friend, Florence Koehler

Dream Valley

from *Three Songs of William Blake*

original key

WILLIAM BLAKE

ROGER QUILTER
Op. 20, No. 1

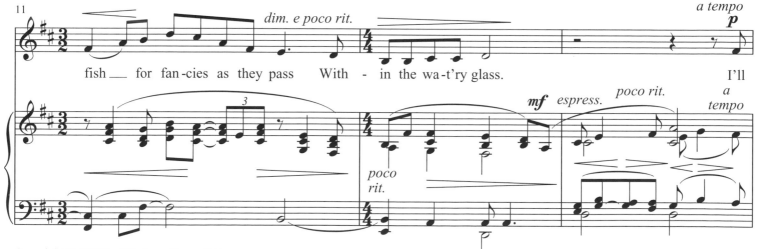

Copyright © 1917 by Winthrop Rogers Ltd.

drink of — the clear — stream, And hear the lin-net's song, And there I'll lie — and dream The

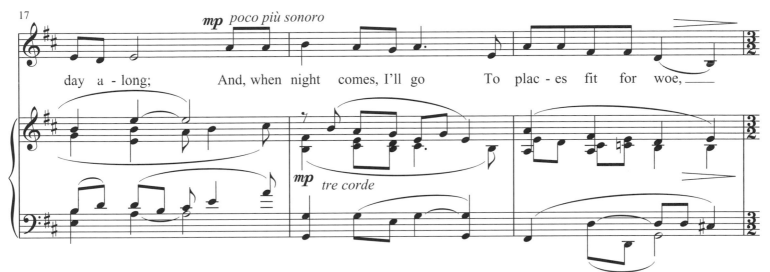

day a - long; And, when night comes, I'll go To plac - es fit for woe,—

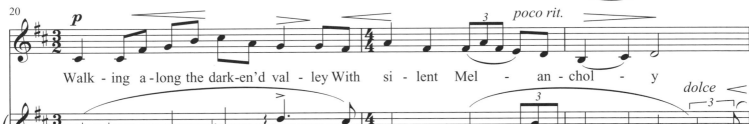

Walk - ing a -long the dark-en'd val - ley With si - lent Mel - an - chol - y

To Gervase Elwes

Love's Philosophy

from *Three Songs*

original key: a minor 3rd higher

PERCY B. SHELLEY

ROGER QUILTER
Op. 3, No. 1

sweet e - mo - tion. No-thing in the world is

sin - gle; All things, by a law di -vine, In one an -

o - ther's be-ing min - gle,— Why not I_____ with

thine, not I,_____ with thine?

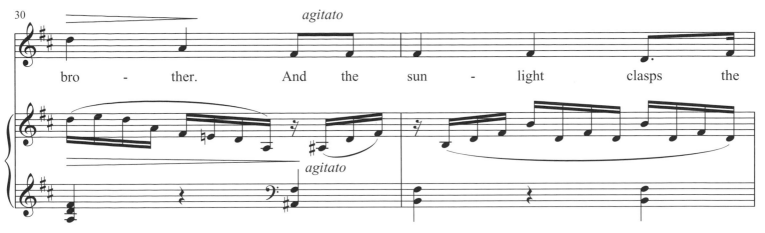

bro - ther. And the sun - light clasps the

earth, And the moon - beams kiss the

sea, _____ What are all these kiss - ings

worth, _____ If

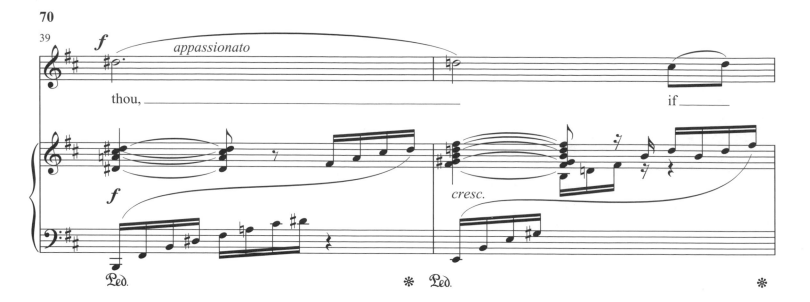

To the memory of my friend, Mrs. Cary-Elwes

Weep you no more

from *Seven Elizabethan Lyrics*

original key: a diminished 4th higher

ANONYMOUS

ROGER QUILTER
Op. 12, No. 1

weep - ing, That now lies sleep - ing, Soft - ly now

soft - ly lies Sleep - ing, sleep - ing.

pp

Sleep is a re-con-ci - ling, A rest that peace be-

gets; *poco cresc.* Doth not the sun rise smil - ing When

fair at even he sets? _____ Rest you, then, rest, sad eyes! Melt not in

weep - ing, While she lies sleep-ing, Soft - ly now

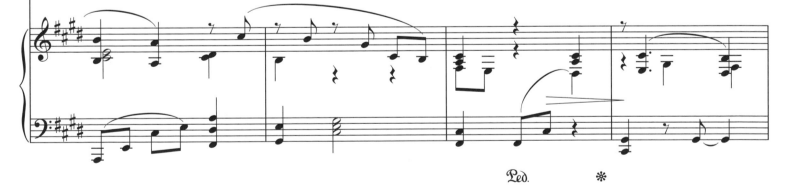

soft - ly lies Sleep - ing, sleep - ing.

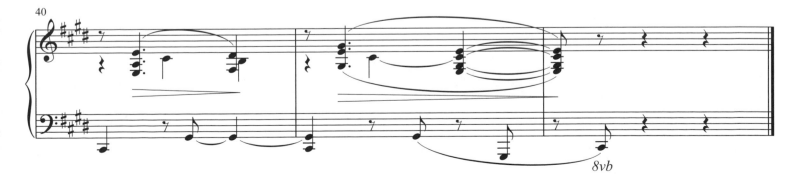

To Nell Tangeman

Little Elegy

original key: a whole step higher

ELINOR WYLIE

NED ROREM

New York City, 28 March 1948
(Spring, cool, bright, noon)

To Shirley Xenia Gabis Rhoads

Love
original key: a major 3rd higher

THOMAS LODGE

NED ROREM

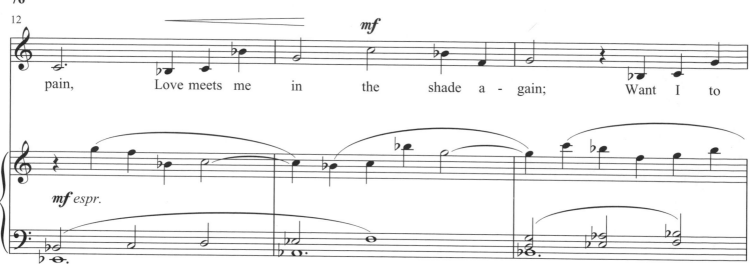

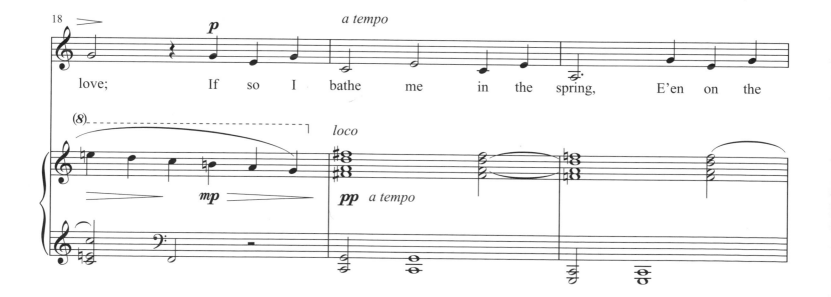

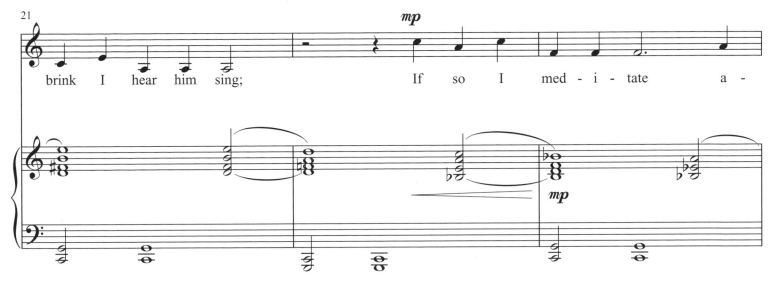

brink I hear him sing; If so I med - i - tate a -

lone, He will be part - ner to my moan; If so I

mourn, he weeps with me, And where I am there will he be.

Hyères, 22 July 1953

A Lullaby

original key: a minor 3rd higher

THOMAS DEKKER
from *Patient Grissel*
(Circa A.D. 1600)

CHARLES VILLIERS STANFORD

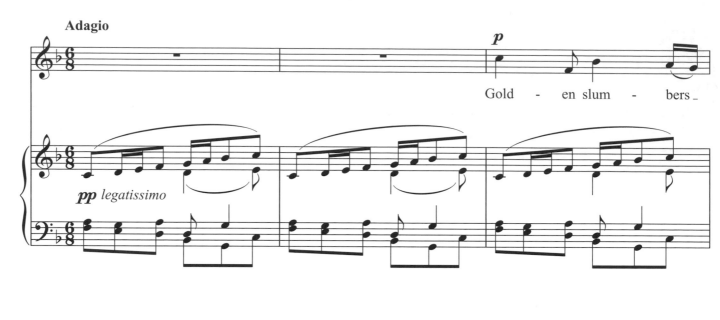

Gold - en slum - bers

kiss __ your eyes, ___ Smiles a - wake you __ when __ you rise, ___

Sleep, pret - ty wan - tons, do not cry, __ And I will sing __ a

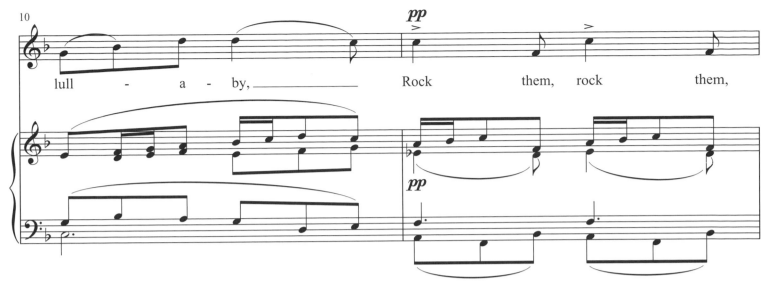

lull - a - by, _____ Rock them, rock them,

lull - a - by. _____

Care is heav - y, ___ there - fore sleep you,

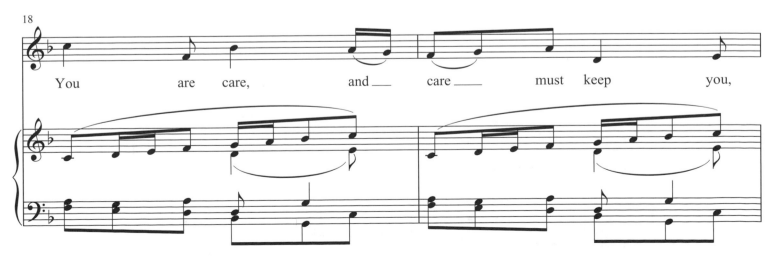

You are care, and ___ care ___ must keep you,

Sleep, pret - ty wan - tons, do not cry, ___ And

I will sing ___ a lull - a - by. ___

Rock them, rock them, lull - a - by. ___

Rock them, rock them, lull - a - by.

Bright is the ring of words

from *Songs of Travel*

original key: a major 2nd lower

ROBERT LOUIS STEVENSON

RALPH VAUGHAN WILLIAMS

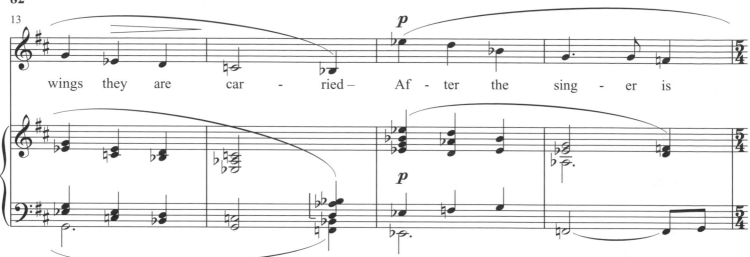

wings they are car - ried— Af - ter the sing - er is

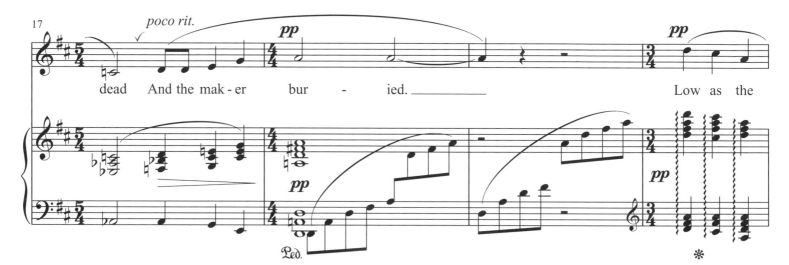

dead And the mak - er bur - ied._____ Low as the

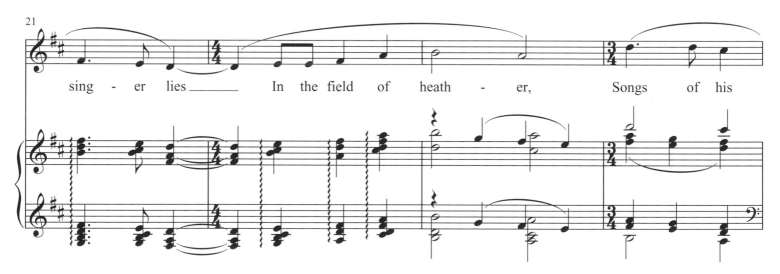

sing - er lies_____ In the field of heath - er, Songs of his

fash - ion bring The swains to - geth - er.

To Mrs. Edmund Fisher

Linden Lea
A Dorset Song
original key

WILLIAM BARNES

RALPH VAUGHAN WILLIAMS

*The original text by William Barnes is in Dorset dialect.
Dorset dialect was spoken in Dorset county in southwestern England.

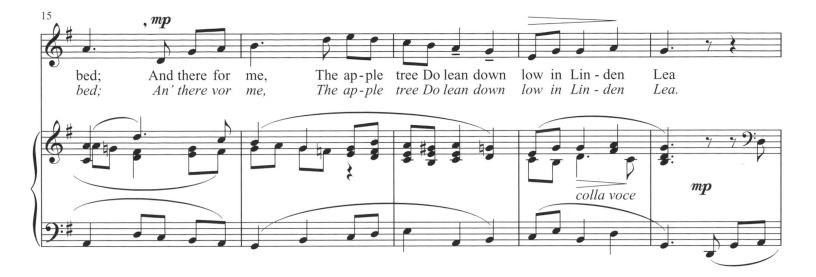

bed;   And there for   me,   The ap-ple   tree Do lean down   low in Lin - den   Lea

bed;   An' there vor   me,   The ap-ple   tree Do lean down   low in Lin - den   Lea.

colla voce   *mp*

When leaves, that late - ly   were a - spring - ing, Now do

When leaves, that lëate - ly   were a - spring - en, Now do

rit.   *a tempo*

fade with - in   the   copse,   And paint - ed   birds   do   hush their sing - ing, Up up -

fade 'ith - in   the   copse,   An' paint - ed   birds   do   hush their zing - en, Up up -

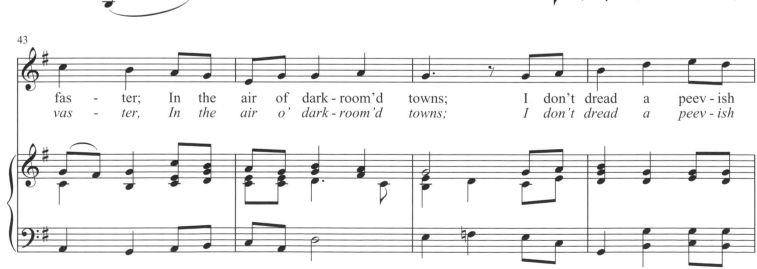

master, Though no man may heed my frowns. I be free to go a-
meäs - ter, Though noo man may heed my frowns. I be free to go a-

broad, Or take a - gain my home - ward road, To where, for me, The ap - ple
brode, Or take a - geän my hwome - ward road, To where, vor me, The ap - ple

tree Do lean down low in Lin - den Lea.
tree Do lean down low in Lin - den Lea.

The sky above the roof

original key

MABLE DEARMER
from the French of Paul Verlaine

RALPH VAUGHAN WILLIAMS

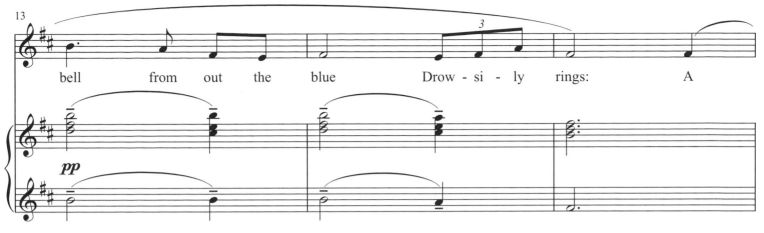

bell from out the blue Drow - si - ly rings: A

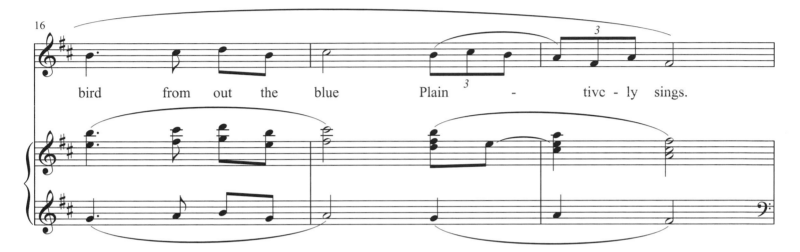

bird from out the blue Plain - tive - ly sings.

Ah God! a life is here, Sim - ple and fair,

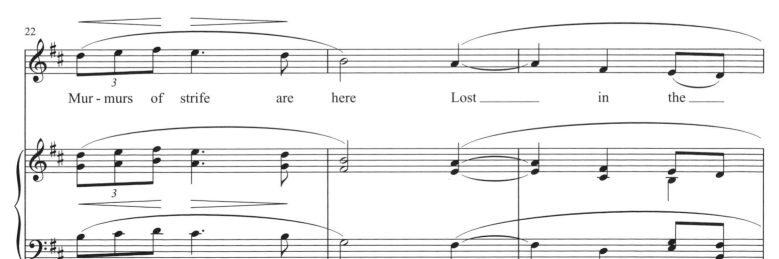

Mur - murs of strife are here Lost _____ in the _____